This Book Is Dedicated With
Heartfelt Thanks
to

Meg Barnhart

Heartfelt Thanks ™

for

Helping kids Love Jesus

Group

Loveland, Colorado

Heartfelt Thanks™ for Helping kids Love Jesus

Visit our Web site: **www.grouppublishing.com**

Credits

Contributing Authors: Raul R. Castañeda, Ellen Javernick, Karol Rarick, Donna Simcoe, and Paul Woods
Editor: Lyndsay E. Gerwing
Creative Development Editor: Mikal Keefer
Chief Creative Officer: Joani Schultz
Copy Editor: Patty Wyrick
Art Director: Jean Bruns
Book Designer/Illustrator: Liz Malwitz Design
Children's Art: Hugh Hart and Mark Malwitz
Cover Art Director: Bambi Eitel
Cover Designer/Illustrator: Marianne Richmond Studio, Inc.
Production Manager: Dodie Tipton

ISBN 0-7644-2638-9
10 9 8 7 6 5 4 3 2   13 12 11 10 09 08 07 06 05 04
Printed in Singapore.

Table of Contents

Introduction

Do you remember the first time you walked into Sunday school? Perhaps you remember clinging to your mother's hand, pleading with her not to leave you. You didn't know anyone. You were frightened to be apart from your parents. But then the teacher came over to you, held out her hand, smiled, and welcomed you to the classroom. You were shy at first, sniffling back tears, afraid of being abandoned. By the end of the first class, you didn't want to leave your new friends and teacher! And you still remember that teacher telling you stories about Jesus from the Bible, helping you in interactive play, and consoling you on that first day.

Thank you

Without people like you, that scared child may never have met God. Thank you for helping children come to know and love Jesus.

Little Treasures

"Goodbye, Nickey," I said as the active five-year-old boy ran out the classroom door. Then I turned my attention to the farewells I had to say to my other students, making sure each child left the room accompanied by the right parent and had his or her correct take-home papers in hand.

"Miss Kay," called a high-pitched young voice. I looked over to see Nickey hadn't left.

"Miss Kay, I love you!" Nickey shouted with a quick wave as he and his dad turned to walk away.

Long after all the goodbyes had been said that morning, I remembered this short phrase of affection from my student. I remembered it the next Sunday when I had to remind Nickey three times to keep his hands to himself during the story time. And I remembered it on the days when he and the other children left without even a wave.

God had given me a little treasure to hold on to, and I stored it in my heart.

♥ Read Psalm 1:3a. What fruits have you seen your children yield? How can you encourage them to continue delighting in the Lord?

♥ Jot down any encouragement you've received teaching Sunday school. Mark passages in this book that have lifted your spirits. Refresh yourself often with them, just as a thirsty man helps himself to a cup of cold water.

4

Dear Lord,
thank you for
encouraging me
to keep teaching
each of the
children you
bring to my
class. May they
always see your
love through me.
Amen.

David and Tavi

Before Brian and I married, we taught fifth- and sixth-graders. Our class included two brothers, David and Tavi.

We wanted children in our class to know they were important to us, so we sent each child a wedding invitation. Our kids weren't just included in their parents' invitations—the kids themselves were invited.

After our honeymoon, we opened gifts. There were many precious remembrances from family and friends. But tucked in a box, carefully wrapped, was one very special gift. David and Tavi had bought us a wedding gift with their own money. It was an inexpensive set of towels, but we cherished the towels as if they were hand-embroidered silk.

♥ Read Mark 10:13-16. How can you invite your church kids into significant moments of your life? How do you think they'd feel? What would they remember?

♥ Celebrate your next birthday or anniversary with your class at church. Bring a cake, and invite your children into your life.

Dear God, thank you for sharing your love with me. Help me to share my life generously with the children in my care. In Jesus' name, amen.

My Journal Response

When you invite children into your life,
they feel important...loved...cherished.

Who has invited you into their lives—
and shared God's love?

Today's date _____

Meant for Me!

As a helper in the kindergarten through first-grade Sunday school class at church, Laura had volunteered to be responsible for preparing the crafts.

Her hand started to feel a little cramped after she had cut out fifteen stars and began writing the main point on each one.

"I'll be so glad when this is finished," she thought. "I wish there weren't so many words to write."

As she continued to mechanically form the letters, her mind wandered to the concerns of her life, and these thoughts plagued her. Suddenly Laura's mind returned to recognize the words she had just written on the last star: "We always WIN when we trust God's plans!"

"Oh, my!" she exclaimed out loud. "This is what I need to learn!"

Laura couldn't wait to tell others. "I thought I was doing these crafts for the children," she said. "Then I realized God intended for me to learn this lesson. I'm so glad I'm working in children's Sunday school because these truths are for me, too!"

♥ Read Hebrews 4:12. How have you seen the Word of God active in children's lives? in yourself?

♥ Let the children see that you are learning with them. Have a memorization contest. Let each person tell what his or her favorite verse is and why—adults included!

8

Dear Lord,
thank you that your Word always speaks truth,
not just to the children, but to my life as well.
Amen.

Mrs. Watson

I was five years old when I first went to church with my parents. That's where I met Mrs. Watson, my Sunday school teacher. She told me God loved me and sent his Son to die for me. Each week she met me with a smile and a hug. I so looked forward to seeing her that I could hardly wait for Sundays to arrive.

Mrs. Watson was in her fifties or sixties then. Now, forty years later, she has probably gone home to be with her Savior, but her loving actions remain with me still. One day I'll see her in heaven—and I'm sure she'll greet me with a smile and a hug.

💜 Consider 3 John 4. How can you show love to children in your class and lead them to Jesus? In what ways do you show children who are new to your class that they're important to you?

💜 Send children in your class notes this week, reminding them that you're praying for them. Kids love getting mail, and you'll be expressing love in a safe, caring way!

Dear Lord, help me find ways to lovingly connect with each child in my care. In Jesus' name, amen.

My Journal Response

Early experiences shape your life—forever.

What's your earliest memory of being in a church building?

Today's date _____

Following the Leader

Not long ago, our church was blessed with a new Spanish-speaking pastor. Word spread quickly, and families of Hispanic origin flocked to our church. Eager to have their children come to know Christ, families enrolled children in a class taught by Pastor Felix, who quickly found he needed sponsors. My Tuesdays were free. I couldn't say no.

Each week Pastor Felix welcomed parents to the adult class in the basement and chatted with children as they headed upstairs for their class.

One Tuesday the children's teacher read aloud a question from the children's workbook: "Who's always there for you in our church?" Several children raised their hands. The teacher called on Raul. Though "Jesus" was the answer written in red ink in the teacher's edition, no one disagreed when Raul responded, "Pastor Felix."

♥ Read Mark 9:37. Do children feel welcomed to your class? What can you do to ensure they feel welcomed?

♥ Think about how you welcome new families to your church. If your congregation has a welcoming committee, ask if your class could make cards to be given to the children of new members.

WELCOME

Dear God,
help me follow Christ's
example, and let me
welcome others into my
faith community with
friendly smiles and kind
words. In Jesus' name,
amen.

Sesame Prayer

My daughter once asked if I was going to "sesame prayer." It took a moment for me to realize that she meant the *intercessory* prayer group I attended.

Young children use words in unique ways. That's why I *love* hearing children pray. They use their own words, praying with honest sincerity and a total lack of pretense.

Listen to the words your children pray at church this week. We can learn from them. We can learn to trust…to believe…to expect answers. Who knows? Perhaps we'll even learn to pray better "sesame prayers" ourselves!

♥ Read Matthew 6:5-15. How can you help your children pray more often? more openly? Who are the children in your life who love to pray? How can you encourage them?
♥ Bring pictures of God's creation to class this Sunday. Invite children to pray aloud, thanking God for the world around them.

Dear God,
thank you for letting me openly and honestly share my heart with you. I love you. In Jesus' name, amen.

"your kingdom come,
your will be done
on earth as it is in heaven."
Matthew 6:10

14

My Journal Response

God wants to hear what's on your heart—what's really on your heart.

What do you want God to know about how you're feeling today?

Today's date _____

Loving Arms

After Sunday school class, David's dad always came to collect him. Though they had been separated for only an hour, the moment David caught sight of his dad in the doorway, he rushed pell-mell into his father's outstretched arms. We all loved to watch their greeting.

We had been working on ways to make God's love real to our little ones. We had taken "wonder walks" to marvel at the way God's love was manifested through his creation. We had celebrated God's gift of Christ at Christmas. Now Easter was upon us. Though we knew the children were too young to understand the crucifixion, we did have an Easter story in our take-home paper. It showed a picture of Christ on the cross.

After looking at the picture for a moment or two, little Molly announced with conviction, "Jesus looks just like David's dad."

I couldn't see even the slightest resemblance. Molly went on, "See, he has his arms out ready to give us a big hug."

♥ Read 1 John 4:12. How can you help your children show God's love to others?

♥ Glue a tiny cross to your mirror so you will be reminded that other people see God through you.

16

Dear Lord,
thank you for being a loving God, the perfect example of how I should treat others.
Help me reflect your love in my relationships with my students and my family.
In Jesus' name, amen.

Stinky Diapers

My husband and I learned an important lesson about God's love from four-year-old Andrew—actually, from Andrew's diapers.

You see, children stayed in our class until they were potty-trained. At four, Andrew still wore diapers. And because he felt self-conscious, he wouldn't tell us when he needed a change—he would hide under a table. Eventually we would catch a whiff of a truly stinky diaper and notice Andrew was nowhere in sight. We would find him and change his diaper, and he would happily go play with the other kids.

Our love for Andrew didn't depend on how he smelled. And that's exactly how God is with us. Because we "stink" of sin, we try to hide. And God's love pursues us, calling us to come to him to be cleaned up.

🤍 Read 1 John 1:9. What sins do you try to hide from God? What sins might your children be hiding? How can you help them ask for God's forgiveness?

🤍 If you occasionally change the diapers of children you serve, remember that your compassionate care reflects God's love.

Dear God, please help me never hide from you. I know you call to me with loving, forgiving words and open arms. In Jesus' name, amen.

My Journal Response

God's love for you depends on his grace—
not your perfection.

How does it feel to be totally,
enthusiastically, wholeheartedly loved?

Today's date _____

Reduced to Its Lowest Form

The concept of the Trinity is a tough one for everybody to grasp. Even St. Patrick was stumped until he came up with the idea of comparing it to a shamrock. Thinking of an analogy that would be appropriate for four-year-olds was a real challenge.

I didn't have much time to do the thinking. My son's family was visiting, and I was doing lesson plans as I fixed Saturday supper for my little granddaughter. Ally, at three, liked a limited number of foods. Stroganoff was not one of them. I'd opted for making her a p.b.j. She was helping! She got the bread from the bag, and with a hand from me, spread the peanut butter. Then she globbed on the jelly and mushed it around a bit with the butter knife. I helped her fold the bread over and, ta-da, a sandwich. Not just a sandwich, but a tasty example of the Trinity. Guess what I served for snacks on Sunday!

♥ Read John 14:16. When have you felt God's unseen presence in your life?
♥ Hold three burning candles together. Notice how the combined flame burns more brightly than the three candles separately. Perhaps God chose to come to us in three forms so we would never miss him in the darkness.

Dear Lord,

thank you for sending us the Holy Spirit.

Help us rely on his guidance as we work with our students.

In the name of the Father, Son, and Holy Spirit,

amen.

God's Gardener

A new little girl, Stacey, came into Lisa's Sunday school class. Lisa encouraged her to join the other children for circle time. After the Bible story, all the children except Stacey jumped to their feet and ran to the next activity.

While Lisa picked up her story materials, Stacey slowly walked over and knelt beside her. "Do you want to look at the pictures in the Bible from our story today?" Lisa asked. Stacey nodded.

When Lisa opened the children's Bible, Stacey said, "My daddy's in jail, and I don't like my mommy's boyfriend." Then she continued on with the sad details of her young life.

"Oh, Jesus," Lisa silently prayed, "she needs you."

"Stacey," Lisa said, "Daddies on earth sometimes make mistakes. But you have a Father in heaven who loves you. He never makes mistakes, and when you believe in his Son, he will never leave you. Jesus will be with you always."

Soon Sunday school was over, and Stacey left the classroom never to return. But the seed of One who would love and care for her forever was planted in Stacey's heart that day.

♥ Read 1 Corinthians 3:6. What seeds have you planted in the hearts of the children you serve? What can you do to ensure you are planting seeds in every child?

♥ Make it a priority to pray that God will bring needy children to your class. Pray also for fertile soil in the hearts of all the children.

My Journal Response

Children's hearts are so often such
receptive soil, and what we plant takes root.

During your childhood, who is someone who
planted a seed that has borne fruit?

Dear Lord,
may no child leave my class without
the seed of eternal life and the love
of Jesus planted in his or her heart.
Amen.

Today's date _____

Teacher Training

I'd always thought of myself as the song and dance queen of Sunday school teachers. I put on puppet shows, did clever crafts, and took field trips…all carefully planned to correlate with the curriculum. But pride goes before a fall.

Last year a new teacher joined the fifth-grade team. Her methods were the antithesis of mine: She was the work sheet queen. I tried to help her out. I enthusiastically shared my ideas with her, but although she thanked me politely, she never used them. Each week her students went home with a boring fill-in-the-blank paper completed in class. One Sunday I could bite my tongue no longer and asked, "Why do you always have the children do work sheets?"

Her answer reminded me that even in teaching religion, one size does not fit all. She pointed to her students, many of whom came from Spanish-speaking homes, and said, "My students use the papers to teach their parents." I realized that Jesus used more than one method to share his message. He was the master of the miracle, a pro at teaching through parables, and a super sermon giver!

"He taught in their synagogues, and everyone praised him."
Luke 4:15

♥ Read Luke 4:15. What methods do you use to teach? Should you consider trying something new?
♥ Write down the names of your students, and consider how each child learns best. Plan next week's lesson to meet their needs.

Dear God, grant me humility. Help me appreciate
different teaching styles as well as different learning styles.
In Jesus' name, amen.

It's Not About Me

The Sunday school director asked Alison to share with the congregation about her class. Alison immediately thought of what she wanted to say. Several of the children had recently responded to God's Word.

But, as the day to speak drew near, Alison grew nervous. "What if I say something wrong and stumble over my words? Or what if I go blank and totally forget what to say?" she fretted.

"Now I wish I hadn't agreed to speak," Alison confided to a friend.

"Alison," her friend said, "it's not about you. It's about God. Those people need to hear the great things he has done with your students. Forget about yourself, and let God use your words to touch hearts."

Although she was still nervous, Alison prayed for God's strength. As she walked up to the podium to speak, she said to herself, "It's not about me. It's about God."

♥ Read Philippians 4:13. What do you need God's strength to help you do this week?
♥ Memorize Psalm 19:14. Say this as a prayer before you teach on Sunday.

Dear Lord, help me remember that this life I live is not about me; it's about you. Amen.

26

My Journal Response

So many words spoken each day…
so few are truly important.

What words do the children you serve most need to hear?
How could you say them?

Today's date _____

Words of Wisdom

The highlight of our vacation Bible school was the "almost overnighter" for our fifth-graders. After our evening activities and just before the parents arrived to take their "campers" home, we had a bonfire in the grassy church courtyard. We brought sticks for our marshmallow roast, and the youth pastor led songs.

Josh rolled his wheelchair into the circle and joined in singing old favorites like "Jacob's Ladder" and "Jesus Loves Me." Someone suggested the silly song "Oh, You Can't Get to Heaven." The kids giggled when they sang, "Oh, you can't get to heaven on roller skates 'cause you'd roll right by those pearly gates," and "Oh, you can't get to heaven in pastor's boat 'cause that rickety thing won't even float." One camper suggested we come up with verses telling how to get to heaven. A hand shot up. While the pastor played chords in the background, a sweet, young voice sang, "Oh, you can get to heaven in Josh's chair because our God welcomes everyone there."

♥ Read John 14:2. Is your view of heaven as all-inclusive as that of your students?

♥ God offers love and forgiveness to everyone. This week think of someone who has hurt or offended you, a friend or family member from whom you've become estranged. Pray for God's help in mending that relationship.

28

"In my Father's house
are many rooms;
if it were not so, I would
have told you.
I am going there to prepare
a place for you."

John 14:2

Dear God, thank you for welcoming everyone to heaven. Help me to be as loving and forgiving of others as you are. In Jesus' name, amen.

Leggo My LEGO

I was a bit nervous the morning I used a learning experience that involved LEGO building blocks with my adult class. One of the class members was Arlene, the seventy-something mother of a theology professor. I wasn't sure how she would respond. I was relieved as most of the class smiled when I distributed the blocks. After they revealed their creations, we had a lively discussion. After class Arlene said to me, "In all my years, that's the most fun I've ever had in an adult Sunday school class!"

♥ Read Philippians 4:4. What does rejoicing have to do with having fun in Sunday school? What long-term effect might having fun in Sunday school have on children? on adults?

♥ This week in class, ask your students what was the most fun they've ever had in a Sunday school class. Take notes on kids' answers, and after class determine what makes class fun for your students. Don't be afraid to let learning be fun!

Dear God,
thanks for bringing joy to our lives! Help me find ways to bring more joy to my students in Sunday school.
In Jesus' name, amen.

"Rejoice in the Lord always I will say again: Rejoice!"

Philippians 4:4

My Journal Response

Children love to have fun—and so do adults.

What's the most fun you've had in church?
What made the experience fun?

Today's date _____

Willing to Listen

When I was a teenager, I went to a church where there was a lot of "telling." We were told how Christian kids should behave, and we were frowned upon if we behaved differently. However, at that church, a middle-aged lady was the youth Sunday school teacher. And she was different from many of the other church leaders. She wanted us to learn to live right, but she was different because she listened. If we came into class with something to discuss—something from the news, a hurt in someone's life, or a question about how the Bible connected with life—she would listen. Sometimes she pointed us to helpful Scriptures. Sometimes she gently gave a bit of advice, but not until she heard all we had to say.

♥ Read Galatians 6:2. Listening means caring and bearing. When has someone really listened to you and helped bear your burdens? How can you help bear the burdens of your class members?

♥ Think right now about a student of yours who is carrying a burden. It might be family struggles, a need for acceptance, or a broken relationship. Give that student a call this week. Ask how things are *really* going. And then listen. If there's anything you can *do* to help bear the burden, do it.

God, thank you for being the chief bearer of our burdens. Help me to really listen and to help bear the burdens my students are carrying. In Jesus name, amen.

"Carry each other's burdens, and in this way

you will fulfill the law of Christ."

Galatians 6:2

The Right Relationships

I remember that Bill was strict with our class of fifth-grade boys. Bill was definitely "old school" and ran a tight ship. However, I ran across a photograph recently that reminded me of what else Bill did. He had class parties. We had game days at the church. We had outdoor parties at his house in the country. He invited us individually to come play with his kids—and to interact with him along the way. He wasn't flashy or smooth, but he had fun with us and got to know us. And he made sure we developed the right relationships—with him, with each other, and with the God he served.

💜 Read John 13:34-35. What's the point Jesus emphasizes? How does that relate to your Sunday school class? How can you demonstrate your love for your students beyond class time?

💜 This week, write notes or e-mails to class members. Let them know you're thinking of them and caring about them. Consider having an event at your home to help you get to know them better.

God,

help me show my

students more of

the love you've

shown to me.

In Jesus' name,

amen.

34

My Journal Response

Ashes to ashes...dust to dust...
What is made for eternity but relationships?

What relationships do you value most?
Why?

Today's date _____

A Little Attention Goes a Long Way!

The first time John and Julie attended our church, I announced that we would have a "birthday party" to celebrate how special God made each of them. John and Julie's parents were so impressed by their children's enthusiasm that they invited my wife and me to their home for dinner. We hadn't done anything out of the ordinary. We just accepted the children and invited them into our family, but it made an incredible difference to them.

Years later I heard that John was still serving God and had joined the Marines. Julie had married a Christian man, and they were serving God together. I can't envision the future for each of my students' lives, but God can.

♥ Read Proverbs 25:11, then Proverbs 8:19. A word spoken at the right time is very powerful and can yield much fruit. What characteristics has God given you that will continue to grow two, five, and ten years down the line?
♥ The next time you have a new student visit your church, give his or her parent a welcome call that week, invite them to your home, or visit them.

Dear God, help me to see and believe in the spiritual future of my students. I will trust you to bring people into my students' lives who will help lead them closer to you. Amen.

"My fruit
is better
than
fine gold;
what
I yield
surpasses
choice
silver."

Proverbs 8:19

What Flashing Lights?

One Sunday Bob and Sarah arrived about ten minutes late to our beginners class. When they came in, their first-grade daughter announced, "We got stopped by a policeman with flashing lights on his car!"

As they drove, Bob and Sarah had been engrossed in the lesson they were going to present and were nearly to the church when they noticed flashing blue lights behind them. The officer informed them that they'd run a stop sign about three miles back, and he'd been following them with lights flashing ever since!

♥ Read 2 Timothy 2:15. What does this verse mean for you and your class? How does God look on our efforts as Sunday school teachers?

♥ This week, try this test: Double your preparation time for Sunday school. If you usually spend half an hour, spend an hour. If you usually spend an hour, spend two hours. Then see how it affects your class time.

God,
thank you for working through me.
Help me to be prepared each week to lead
the lesson you want for your children.
In Jesus' name, amen.

38

My Journal Response

When flashing lights don't get your attention, you're just too busy.

How would you rate your "busyness"— too much, not enough, or just about right? Why?

Today's date _____

Dear God,
thank you for sending
Christian men and women
into my life. Help me to
embrace the spiritual
responsibility to mentor
the children with whom you
bless me. Amen.

I Serve Today Because of You

My parents didn't take me to church, so I was a "special events only" child. When a neighbor invited me to a Sunday school contest or picnic, I'd show up—excited to be included.

That is, I was excited until a teacher told us that we should all attend each week, not just for special events.

That stung. I couldn't drive to church. I didn't have any way to get there each week.

So I quit going at all.

Then a man from the church took it upon himself to offer me a ride to church. He met with my parents. He got to know my siblings. He became my "spiritual father" in a way my own dad couldn't be…at first.

You see, this man's steady involvement in my life led not just to my being involved in church. It also led to my parents going…and my brother going…and my sisters going. It led to my own father learning to be the spiritual man who could lead his family in the ways of God.

♥ Read Mark 10:14. How do you show your students that they can come to you and feel God's love?

♥ If possible, look up a previous Sunday school teacher, pastor, or youth worker who impacted your life. Give that person a surprise phone call, send a card, or send an e-mail. Thank the person for the times you remember he or she showed love and acceptance toward you. Even if the person doesn't remember you, you will be a blessing to him or her for months or years to come.

My Journal Response

People tell us they love us, and we appreciate it.
People show us, and it changes us—forever.

Who is showing you love? How?
How does it feel?

Today's date _____

Just a Hat

Danny had just made a faith commitment and was breaking away from a gang. His only hat bore his gang's colors and markings. The youth teacher suggested that a few guys go with Danny to buy a more appropriate hat. It seemed dangerous to have our son Josh out in public with this ex-gang member. With trepidation, we allowed Josh to go. Danny got a new hat, and life went on.

Two years later, Danny told Josh how much it had meant for those guys to go with him that night. Their actions had proven to him that he'd made the right choice in following Jesus. The Holy Spirit was working that night, and I'm sure glad we didn't get in the way!

♥ Put on some lively music, and tap your foot with the music. Then turn off the volume for thirty seconds, but keep your foot tapping "in step" with the music. Turn the music back on, and see how you did.

♥ Read Galatians 5:25. How is trying to keep in step with the volume turned off like trying to follow Jesus without listening for the Holy Spirit's promptings?

Dear God, help me follow the thoughts I know are from you as I lead my class. In Jesus' name, amen.

43

The Faith of a Child

As the song came to an end, I asked the children, "How has God helped you this week?"

With a look of worry and concern, little Josh said, "God helped my mother get up when she fell down." You see, Josh's young mom has had severe back trouble for many years and was now using a cane.

My preschoolers prayed for her. I later took the opportunity to tell Josh's mom that her son showed his love for her by asking us to pray for her during class. We talked. She shared, and we prayed together that God would continue to heal her back so she could care for her son.

♥ Read 1 Peter 5:7. What are some of the cares or anxieties that your children express? What are some of the worries you have when it comes to teaching the children in your class?

♥ List or draw pictures of each of your worries on sticky notes. Get a heavy blanket, fold it, and place it around your neck. As you pray, pick up each sticky note, say the worry, and attach it to the blanket. When you finish asking God to take care of your worries, experience the sensation of relief as you remove the blanket and your cares are lifted away.

Lord,
thank you for building a faith in your little ones that transcends our adult minds.
Continue to use them to remind us that you care for every person in their lives.
Amen.

"Cast all your anxiety on him because he cares for you."

1 Peter 5:7

Never Give Up

Dan wasn't interested in the faith his parents had found. They forced him to come to Sunday school, and everyone knew he didn't want to be there. I made Dan my personal project. I'd drop over after school and shoot baskets. I'd invite him to events I knew he'd like. I didn't pressure him, but I let him know that I wanted him to consider Jesus. After three years, Dan turned his life over to Jesus. Afterward, Dan looked at me and said, "Well, God finally got to me. Thanks for not giving up!"

♥ Read Luke 11:5-10. What does this passage say about our persistence as Sunday school teachers? Think about a difficult student. How might your persistence pay off in teaching and praying?

♥ Take sixty seconds to shape a lump of modeling clay into the form of a person. Use as much time as you need to form a person from another lump. When you've finished, compare your two sculptures. How did your persistence pay off?

God, help me to be persistent in reaching out to my students and in bringing their needs before you. In Jesus' name, amen.

My Journal Response

No matter where you work with children, there's usually one child who's a challenge to love.

Who is someone who never gave up on you?

Today's date _____

Planting Seeds of Faith

The heart-wrenching answer to the question "What do you want God to do for you or someone else this week?" came as my co-teacher and I finished Circle Time at the Christian school where I taught.

"I want God to help my parents stop fighting" came the reply. Lelani was only five. My co-teacher and I managed somehow to get through the prayer time as we tried desperately to hide our emotions.

The next day Lelani ran up to me with a big smile on her face and quietly said, "My mom and dad didn't fight." Lelani knew God had answered her prayers for that day, and I did too!

♥ Read Matthew 13:31-32. What are some seeds of faith that God has planted in your heart? How have they grown your faith to what it is today?

♥ Fill a large, clear jar to the top with water. Set the jar on a table in front of you. As the water is still swirling slightly, add one drop of blue food coloring and watch how it spreads down into the bottom of the jar. As you meditate on God's faithfulness in your life, notice how the color seems to form branches as it grows, much like a tiny mustard seed grows into a large, strong plant.

Dear God, forgive my unbelief,
and plant your simple faith in my heart, too. Amen.

49

My Journal Response

Every child has a name, a face, and a heritage.
No two children are alike.

Who was an adult who saw you for who
you are when you were a child?
How did that feel?

Today's date _____

Whatever You Do...

My mother's preparation for Sunday school classes was an almost-every-evening thing. And she'd pray for her class members—every day. My mom's favorite verse was Colossians 3:23, and she lived by that verse in every part of her life—including her teaching.

My mom passed away a few years ago. Among her belongings we found a journal that included things about children she had prayed for and taught and newspaper clippings announcing their weddings and awards. In heaven I'm sure my mom will have dozens rejoicing with her because of the impact she had in their lives.

♥ Read Colossians 3:23. How might your teaching better honor the Lord you serve?

♥ Create a little sign with the words, "Who am I working for?" Place it where you'll see it often. Every time you look at the card, think about the question. At the end of the week, think about how that question changed things you did.

Dear God, help me always keep my focus on you and on why I'm teaching. In Jesus' name, amen.

A Christian's Challenge

When Aaron first came to our drop-in center, he didn't fit in with the other street-smart kids. Whenever we had large group activities, Aaron would refuse to be a part of them. One day our "rap session" ended early, so I decided to take the boys out for a game of touch football. To my surprise, Aaron didn't hesitate to join a team and ended up catching many of the scoring points. Football was Aaron's comfort zone.

The challenge to help kids build relationships is ever-present in my ministry. On the hard days, I am reminded that God's power is always present. God is always proving his faithfulness when I don't give up on a child with a challenge.

💜 Read Hebrews 10:23-25. Remind yourself of why you teach children. What are some challenges you have in the classroom? What are some things you can do to encourage your students and yourself?

💜 Choose a child in your class who poses a challenge. Commit to praying for him or her. Make it a point to call or visit that student. Get permission from the parent to take him or her for a soda or ice cream or just to toss a ball back and forth at the local park or in front of the child's home.

Dear God, help me to reach out to even the most challenging students.
I know you brought them to me for a purpose—
to impact my life and to make a difference in theirs. Amen.

"And let us consider how we may
Spur one another on toward
love and good deeds."
Hebrews 10:24

I Don't Sing—I Sit Down

One day as I was driving with my young son in the car, I said, "Tell me what you like about Sunday school, son."

"My friends sing 'Jesus Loves Me.' I don't sing. I sit down," he said. I knew how typical this was.

"Do you like to hear the songs?" Glancing at him through the rearview mirror, I saw him give a simple nod. The conversation was over, and I was relieved!

The following Sunday I peeked through the window of his classroom. This time I knew that, even though he was sitting down, the Holy Spirit was speaking to his little heart, regardless of his level of participation.

♥ Read Isaiah 55:10-11. What purpose do you see God accomplishing in the lives of your students?
♥ This week when you water your lawn or see the rain or snow falling, realize that God touches your students' lives in different ways. Then remember that God will continue to "water" each life in his timing and in his way.

"As the rain and the snow come down from heaven...
Isaiah 55:10a

Dear God, thank you for placing [student's name] in my class. Help me to say the right words that water [his or her] heart. Thank you for the promise that your Word will not return empty. Amen.

My Journal Response

A shrug. A nod. A "yeah—whatever."
Kids who don't respond drive us to distraction.

But our words do matter because God's truth
is in them. What's something you heard as a child
that you didn't understand until years later?

Today's date _____

I'm Not a Preacher

Mr. Teeters called himself a "country boy," but he lived in the big city like me. He would always say, "I'm not a preacher." But in my young mind, he was the best "preacher" I had ever heard! He taught us how to survive in God's country—something I knew nothing about growing up in the barrio of San Jose. He taught us life skills and how to make friends. He taught us discipline and took us camping. Every meeting Mr. Teeters told us that Jesus loved us.

After only a few meetings, I decided that I, too, wanted to follow Jesus, like he did. Mr. Teeters proved that Jesus loved us by loving us first. He may not have seen himself as a preacher, but he preached loud and clear that Jesus loved me and that I needed to love others. Thanks to Mr. Teeters, I continue to "preach" God's practical love to boys and girls who want to change the world for Jesus.

♥ Read Matthew 28:18-20. What are the "life skills" you're good at that might draw people to Jesus?
♥ Talk to your children's director or pastor, and ask for permission to have a class potluck at the local park. Keep it very simple so you can focus on meeting and getting to know your students' parents.

Dear God,
thanks for the Mr. Teeters that you send into our lives.
Help us to draw from them your wisdom and power to change our
students' lives for your kingdom. Amen.

He Knows the Life That's Touched

From the time we first began renting her elementary school, Arial was there. Each Sunday night one of our teachers walked her home. Sometimes Mom was there, sometimes a baby sitter. Arial would suggest songs, ask to pray, bring friends, and participate with an enthusiasm that most of the time surpassed our "churched" kids. Seven months later, Arial announced she had to move.

Yes, we made a difference in her life, but more important, God used Arial to engrave in our memories that every child who enters our church doors is precious and has only a short time with us. God knows the lives we touch, and God knows the children that will cause our characters to be changed.

♥ Read Mark 1:41. How has Jesus touched your life with compassion? How can you touch the lives of your children?

♥ Reflect on the memories of students who have impacted your life. Draw individual pictures of those children. Then place the pictures in your Bible as a reminder to pray for God to continue to guide each child's life and bring him or her closer in relationship with him.

Dear God, continue to change me into the teacher you want me to be. I want to touch more children's lives. Thank you, God, for loving my children and me. Amen.

My Journal Response

It's the words shared as the front door hangs open, just before one friend walks out into the night to return home, that mean the most. Words like "I love you," and "Call anytime," and "Come back soon."

What are the last words you'd like to share with the children you serve? Why don't you say them first?

Today's date _____

Happy Gregory Day!

G

Gregory came to our church each week in a wheelchair. He had multiple sclerosis. Gregory would sit enthusiastically in the front row, listening as I taught the Bible story and participating as much as he could. We prayed for him and accepted him.

One particular Sunday, Gregory's mom came in so excited! Gregory had gotten out of his wheelchair and used his canes as his doctor and she had encouraged him to do for so long. To many, Gregory's healing may not be a miracle. But to the rest of the children in class, God showed his power in a miraculous way that day. Even months later, the children referred to that day as "Happy Gregory Day!"

♥ Read Matthew 9:4-8. Reflect on ways you and your students can show acceptance and love to others who might be different. How do you celebrate the children's accomplishments?

♥ Celebrate your children's accomplishments. Have noisemakers available for children to blow when others share how they encouraged a friend that week or obeyed their parents.

Dear God, help me believe in your power to heal whether it's mental, physical, or spiritual. Remind me to encourage celebration for all that my children accomplish. Amen.

Make Room for Johnny

Johnny was special. He was autistic. Johnny never spoke; he just sat in his own little world. He required a one-on-one helper to guide him through the Bible story time, as did most of the children in our special needs class.

Johnny may never know that he touched and blessed so many lives. We were blessed, not because he spoke to us and told us we were a blessing to him or even that he responded during the Bible stories, but because of the special boy he was. We made room for Johnny and the other special children God sent us, and God made room for us to grow and change into the teachers and volunteers he wanted us to become.

♥ Read Hebrews 13:1-2. How are you meeting the needs of the children in your class? Are there areas of need that could be better met?
♥ Find a ministry partner, and begin praying and asking God to bring a vision and solution for that child or group of children. Watch God change the class!

Dear God, help me to make room for the Johnnys that come into my life. Help me to continue to teach them your love with enthusiasm, whether they respond each week or not. Remind me to pray for each of my children daily, and teach me how to show them that they are a blessing to me and to our church. Amen.

"keep on loving each other as brothers. Do not forget to entertain strangers, for by so doing some people have entertained angels without knowing it."

Hebrews 13:1-2

Thank You